LIMESTONE AND OTHER SEDIMENTARY ROCKS

Nancy Kelly Allen

PowerKiDS press

New York

For Nick

Published in 2009 by The Rosen Publishing Group, Inc.
29 East 21st Street, New York, NY 10010

First Edition

Editor: Amelie von Zumbusch
Book Design: Kate Laczynski
Photo Researcher: Jessica Gerweck

Photo Credits: Cover, pp. 1, 4, 10, 12, 14, 16, 18, 20 Shutterstock.com; p. 6 © Mark Douet/Getty Images; p. 8 © Jeff Foott/Getty Images.

Library of Congress Cataloging-in-Publication Data

Allen, Nancy Kelly, 1949–
   Limestone and other sedimentary rocks / Nancy Kelly Allen. — 1st ed.
      p. cm. — (Rock it!)
   Includes bibliographical references and index.
   ISBN 978-1-4358-2759-2 (lib. bdg.) — ISBN 978-1-4358-3182-7 (pbk.)
ISBN 978-1-4358-3188-9 (6-pack)
   1. Rocks, Sedimentary—Juvenile literature. 2. Limestone—Juvenile literature. I. Title.
   QE471.A5598 2009
   552'.5—dc22
                              2008031798

Manufactured in the United States of America

CONTENTS

You can see layers of sedimentary rock that formed over millions of years at Utah's Bryce Canyon National Park.

A Rocky Start

Have you ever broken a rock? Every day, natural forces break rocks into smaller rocks. Forces such as wind and rushing water wear away bits of rock. These small pieces of rock are known as sediment. Over time, sediment builds up and forms **layers**. After millions of years, layers of sediment pile high. Sediment is heavy and packs together. Under **pressure**, the packed layers change into sedimentary rock.

Sedimentary rocks also form from sediment that is not made up of rocks. **Minerals** that are **dissolved** in water can form sedimentary rock. Sedimentary rock even forms from animal remains! For example, the sedimentary rock limestone is made of the remains of sea animals.

This girl is looking at a marble statue. Marble is a metamorphic rock made from the sedimentary rock limestone.

Breaking into Pieces

Sedimentary rock covers most of Earth's surface. The other two kinds of rocks that make up Earth are igneous rocks and metamorphic rocks.

In time, one kind of rock can change into another. Many of the bits of sediment that make up sedimentary rock come from metamorphic rocks and igneous rocks. Heat and pressure under ground can change sedimentary rocks and igneous rocks into metamorphic rocks. Very deep under ground, all rocks become so hot that they melt. This melted rock, which is called magma, forms igneous rock when it cools and hardens. The making and remaking of rocks is called the rock cycle.

Sedimentary rocks with large grains are called conglomerates. You can still recognize the pieces of old rock in a conglomerate.

Bits and Pieces

Most sedimentary rocks are made up of pieces of old rocks. These sedimentary rocks are known as clastic rocks. Clastic rocks are made up of bits of rock, called clasts or grains, that are held together by a mix of mineral **crystals**, known as cement.

Clastic rocks are grouped by the size and shape of their grains. Clay is the smallest grain size, followed by silt, and then sand. Pebbles, cobbles, and boulders are larger grains. Some clastic rocks, such as sandstone, have only grains that are the same size. Other clastic rocks are made up of large grains and small grains mixed together.

Sandstone comes in different colors, depending on what minerals were in the sand from which it formed. If the sand had iron, the sandstone is yellow, orange, or reddish.

Sticking Together

There are many kinds of clastic rocks. Breccia is made of pieces of rocks with sharp edges that are cemented together. Small-grained clay and mud form a clastic rock called shale. Mud and clay often mix together in layers in calm waters, such as lakes. When the heavy upper layers press water out of the lower layers, shale forms.

Grains of sand form sandstone. Sandstone that formed in deserts usually has thicker layers and smoother grains than sandstone that formed in rivers. Many deserts are home to strange and beautiful landforms made of sandstone.

Cathedral Rock, in Arizona, is a giant red landform made of sandstone. This rock got its name because it is shaped somewhat like a cathedral, or large church.

Often, a stalagmite forms directly below a stalactite. If the stalactite and stalagmite grow enough, they will meet in the middle to form a column.

Drip Drop

There are other types of sedimentary rocks besides clastic rocks. For example, chemical sedimentary rocks form when water passing over rocks dissolves and carries away some of the minerals in those rocks. When the water dries up, the minerals are left behind. Over time, these minerals build up and form chemical sedimentary rocks.

If you have visited a cave, you may have seen chemical sedimentary rock formations called **stalactites** and **stalagmites**. These are often formed by water dripping through limestone rock. Stalactites hang from the top of a cave. Stalagmites rise up from a cave's floor.

Kentucky's Mammoth Cave is home to Frozen Niagara, a group of stalactites and stalagmites. The stalactites and stalagmites are so long that they join together. They look like the famous waterfall Niagara Falls.

The chalk that makes up the white cliffs of Dover is made from the bodies of coccoliths. Coccoliths were algae, or plantlike living things.

From Life to Rocks

Biologic sedimentary rocks form from the remains of plants and animals that lived long ago. Limestone is a biologic sedimentary rock made from the shells and bones of ocean animals. Over time, the shells and bones of these animals build up on the ocean floor in layers. The layers press together and form limestone rock. Limestone is made of a mineral called calcite. Calcite is also known as lime. That is how limestone gets its name.

Chalk is a soft kind of limestone rock made of **crushed** bodies of tiny sea animals. The white cliffs of Dover, in England, are made of chalk. They formed millions of years ago, when dinosaurs lived on Earth.

Layers even form in sedimentary rocks of the same kind. You can see several layers of limestone at Jasper National Park, in Alberta, Canada.

Bottom to Top

Much of Earth is covered with layers of sedimentary rock. Often, each layer is made of a different kind of sedimentary rock. This may produce layers of different colors. The layers are usually flat and **horizontal**. However, flowing water, wind, or movement in Earth's crust can cause these layers to move and make them lie at an angle.

New layers of sedimentary rock form on top of old ones. Therefore, the lower layers of rock are usually older than the upper layers. When rocks are cut to build highways through mountains, you can see layers of rock that go back **billions** of years.

Arizona's Grand Canyon displays striped layers of sandstone, shale, and other sedimentary rocks. The bottom layer is over 2 billion years old. The top layer is about 260 million years old.

The fossils of animals that lived in water, such as this crustacean, are often found in the sedimentary rocks shale and limestone.

Clues in Fossils

Some layers of sedimentary rock hold fossils, or the remains of plants and animals that lived long ago. Fossils form in several ways. Sometimes, water washes away the soft body parts of animals that have died. Sediment covers the hard parts, such as bones and shells. In time, minerals from the sediment may take the place of the minerals in these hard body parts. Sediment also forms **molds** of shells or bones. Plants can become fossils, too. Mud hardens around plants to form fossils.

Fossils help us understand how life on Earth has changed over time. They offer clues about when and where animals and plants lived.

More than 90 percent of the coal mined in the United States is burned to produce electricity. Coal is also used in making tar, plastic, and steel.

The Power of the Stone

Coal and oil are **fuels** that form in sedimentary rock. As fossils did, these fuels began forming millions of years ago from dead plants and animals. Oil comes from small sea animals that were buried in sediment at the bottoms of oceans soon after they died. In time, these animals' bodies become oil and the sediment around them becomes sedimentary rock.

Coal forms from rotting plants that once grew in watery areas. Both coal and oil are burned to produce power that heats and cools buildings and makes lights, stoves, TVs, and other useful things work.

Can you believe it? Your toothbrush is made from oil. The paint on your wall, the gas that runs your car, and anything made of plastic are made from oil, too.

Cut in Stone

How important are sedimentary rocks? We use these rocks every day. Sandstone and limestone are cut into blocks for building. The **pyramids** of Giza, in Egypt, were built of sandstone and limestone over 3,500 years ago and are still standing! Sandstone is also ground up to make glass. We use glass to make windows, drinking glasses, and many other things.

Sedimentary rocks hold fuels that are used to power our world. These rocks and the fossils in them also provide a record of life on Earth. Many of the first tools that human beings created were made from the sedimentary rock chert. Today, we have found many more uses for these rocks.

GLOSSARY

billions (BIL-yunz) Thousands of millions. One billion is 1,000 million.

crushed (KRUSHD) Destroyed by pressing.

crystals (KRIS-tulz) Hard, clear matter that has points and flat sides.

dissolved (dih-ZOLVD) Mixed totally into a liquid.

fuels (FYOOLZ) Things used to make warmth or power.

horizontal (hor-ih-ZON-til) Going from side to side.

layers (LAY-ers) Thicknesses of something.

minerals (MIN-rulz) Natural things that are not animals, plants, or other living things.

molds (MOHLDZ) Hollow forms in special shapes.

pressure (PREH-shur) A force that pushes on something.

pyramids (PEER-uh-midz) Large, stone structures with square bottoms and triangular sides that meet at a point on top.

stalactites (stuh-LAK-tyts) Creations made by water and rock that hang down from the roofs of caves. They can be shaped like icicles.

stalagmites (stuh-LAG-myts) Creations made by water and rock that rise up from the ground.

INDEX

WEB SITES

Due to the changing nature of Internet links, PowerKids Press has developed an online list of Web sites related to the subject of this book. This site is updated regularly. Please use this link to access the list:
www.powerkidslinks.com/rockit/limestone/